HID-IN-Life™ series

PORN

Addiction Recovery Booklets

HID-IN-Life™ series

PORN

Addiction Recovery Booklets

Dr. George T. Crabb, D.O.
Steven B. Curington

A SPECIAL THANKS to the RU editorial team for tirelessly working to produce this product with us:
Donna Bowman, Carolyn Curington, Joy Kingsbury, Kay Niederwerfer.

Design and Layout: Jeremy N. Jones

REFORMERS UNANIMOUS INTERNATIONAL

PO Box 15732, Rockford, IL 61132
Visit our website at www.reformu.com.
Printed in Canada
Cover design by Jeremy N. Jones

                     Crabb, Dr. George T., 1965-
                     Curington, Steven B., 1965-
Porn
ISBN 978-1-60702-973-1

TABLE OF CONTENTS

Addiction: medically speaking from a biblical perspective

The enormous question that faces us today is this: "Is addiction a disease?" The answer is: NO! Addiction is not a disease. But, it is a disorder. It is a disorder that can make you very sick both physically and spiritually. It is also the reason why many contract diseases. The disorder of addiction is brought on by *a* bad choice that is followed by many other bad choices.

I like to formally define addiction as "something I continue to do, even though I know it is bad for me." My friend, if you know it is bad for you, and you continue to do it, then you have a full fledged addiction. This disorder caused by addiction is a self-induced disorder of the brain. It is brought on when an individual improperly uses chemical substances and/or destructive behaviors as coping mechanisms to deal with the pain, uncertainty, disappointments, loss, and other like traumas in life.

As this behavior is repeated, physiological changes eventually occur in the brain. These changes further enhance the disorder and compel the individual to use the substance and/or destructive behavior with greater frequency and intensity. Eventually, the behavior leads to more pain, frustration, fear, uncertainty, and disappointment. The individual becomes trapped in a vicious cycle with unresolved pain as a result of engaging destructive coping mechanisms that were initially meant to alleviate the pain.

Addiction is a process that starts with a choice. That choice allows the manipulation of neurotransmitters (chemical messengers in the brain). However, through manipulation of these "feel goods," they are eventually depleted. This results in devastating destruction, depression, and ultimately death. Thus, the chasing of the "high" ends up being a futile struggle to maintain normality.

Addiction often finds its origin in a sense of personal dissatisfaction. Disappointment, anger, resentment, low self-esteem, rejection, and a host of other negative perceptions can lead an individual to search for redemption and relief in drugs, alcohol, and other self-destructive behaviors. At first, the individual discovers that the chemical or behavior not only offers relief from negative feelings, but it also offers a temporary sense of control and power.

Once the destructive behavior becomes a habit, however, the user quickly loses control and becomes the victim. Physically and emotionally dependent as well as spiritually bankrupt, the individual becomes virtually enslaved to the substance or behavior.

Because of the spiritual and emotional root causes of substance abuse and destructive behavior, along with the physical sequelae, the path to recovery must involve both spiritual, emotional, and physical correction and healing.

A life broken by substance abuse can be rebuilt, and an individual can emerge a stronger person. But, it is going to take the Truth! This book seeks to explain to you to the medical truth of your addiction, while at the same time introducing you to the spiritual Truth which will strengthen you out of your world of despair.

It is our wish that the Truth will make you free, that you may be FREED INDEED!

RU tired? If so, try RU! At Reformers Unanimous International Addictions Program, we strive to help everyone find freedom from stubborn habits and addictions introducing them to the only Truth that makes free—Jesus Christ.

But, many other people do the same type of thing. They say, "Try Jesus!" But, after you give Him a try, they are nowhere to be found. If you are going to "give Jesus a try," you must have support to strengthen you in your trials. For to "try Jesus" as they often say, is to be "tried by Jesus."

You see, life is full of trials and turmoil. It is these trials that lead many of us to find a drug of choice to avoid the reality of life. But, there is a better way! Jesus longs to save you from this world and all its various vices. He wants to not only face your trials *with* you, He wants to face your trials *for* you!

Some think religion is a crutch. Well, if something is broken, it needs a crutch to support it while it strengthens. That is what we seek to do at RU. We seek to support you as God strengthens you over your many weaknesses in life.

I don't want you to try Jesus. Rather, I want you to just stop trying! Let God do the work in your life. He has a wonderful plan for you! My co-author and friend, Dr George Crabb, and I want to reveal that wonderful plan to you in this book.

If you are attending or would like to attend one of our hundreds of meetings that are held weekly throughout the world, we will commit to support you like a crutch. After all, that is what religion is supposed to be—God's support group. God's support system and its body of believers is found within good local churches. Every RU program in America meets in a local church or is sponsored by a local church. For this reason, we can commit to you that when you come to an RU program, you will be met by people who love God, who know God, and who are willing to serve you on behalf of God.

Below is a list of ways in which we at RU will support you as God empowers you to overcome your stubborn habits or addictions. Welcome to a ministry that has as its primary purpose love and support as you gain victory over life's vices.

THE RUI MINISTRIES STUDENT SUPPORT SYSTEM

Stories of Victory: RU tired of hearing the "war stories" of people who have no real freedom in their life? **If so, try RU!** Every week, our students share how God has changed their lives through real-life, relevant stories. This weekly forty minutes of encouraging testimonies will get your weekend started off just right.

Great Teaching: RU tired of talking about problems and doing nothing about them? **If so, try RU!** Every RU class ends with a 30-minute teaching lesson that exposes valuable Bible principles that are integral to your recovery process.

Complete Curriculum: RU tired of being told what is right and not being given the tools to determine what is right? **If so, try RU!** We have one of the best comprehensive discipleship curriculums in America. It is one of the best selling, too! Thousands of people have used our curriculum to learn the Truth about addictions and Christian apathy.

Motivational Awards: RU tired of trying to find the stamina to do the right thing in the face of mounting adversity? **If so, try RU!** We will not only encourage you and help you to do the right thing, but we will also motivate you to do so. Though an award system is just a small way of doing this, it is evidence of a program that believes in acknowledging accomplishment and rewarding participation.

Free Personal Counseling: RU tired of having to get advice from people who know little about your struggles? RU tired of having to pay hourly fees to hear yourself talk? **If so, try RU!** We offer free group and individual spiritual counseling on a wide variety of topics from addiction, to marriage, finances, family, and many other areas. You will have a leader, a helper, a director, and even the pastor available as your own personal counselors during times of urgent need.

Well-Trained Local Leadership Staff: RU tired of attending programs where the leaders and volunteer workers have the same problems as you? **If so, try RU!** Our leaders have been made free from the power of sin and can openly speak about it. They do not seek anonymity. They earnestly proclaim that Jesus is the reason for their freedom, and they have been well trained to use our program and its tools to get that salvation message to you and to those whom you love.

Exciting Children's Program: RU tired of trying to find someone to help you with your child's issues while you are still trying to deal with your many issues in life? **If so, try RU!** We will not only care for your children while you attend your class, but we will entertain, teach, and develop your children. We want them to avoid the same pitfalls that ensnared many of us. They will enjoy games, prizes, snacks, play time, awards, great teaching, and many other things. Our "Kidz Club" is the weekly highlight of every child that attends.

Clean, Well-Staffed Nurseries: RU tired of programs that will not care for your little ones? **If so, try RU!** Those programs say "come as you are." But, you "are" a family; you should be able to come "as a family." If churches can offer free nurseries, then why can't an addiction program? Our clean nurseries are well staffed by volunteers of the hosting church. These volunteers have been screened and trained; and they will love your children because they love children!

Free Transportation: RU tired of trying to find a ride to places that are wanting to and waiting to help you? **If so, try RU!** We want to pick you up and will do so for almost every one of our weekly meetings, if necessary. Though some exceptions may apply, our trained drivers are here for those of you who may be without a car or license. No questions will be asked, except your address, of course!

Weekly Fellowship Time: RU tired of being alone absent of any good friends with whom you could fellowship? **If so, try RU!** RU offers its own "Happy Hour" fellowship time at the conclusion of Friday meetings. As well, our Sunday and mid-week meetings usually offer multiple opportunities to fellowship with your fellow students and leaders. Fellowship is "R" specialty; what about "U"? Then join RU! Visitors, the *RU Happy Hour* is an optional part of our Friday night class. Refreshments and food are usually served, and served well.

Residential Treatment Centers: RU tired of trying to find residential treatment that is effective and affordable? **If so, try RU!** We operate a beautiful 100-bed facility for men and a gorgeous 40-bed facility for women at our headquarters in Rockford, Illinois. This program boasts an over 90% success rate among its graduates. We are also aware of many RU type transitional homes that may be available for your use. Please visit **www.ruhomes.org** to learn more information about our homes and to download an application.

Multi-Meeting Assemblies Weekly: RU tired of not being able to find a meeting when you need one? **If so, try RU!** We offer two to three meetings every weekend and even some during the week. Plus, we offer many activities and service opportunities for our students. Please see your RU director to find the times and days of our meetings and the hosting church's service times.

Local Church Support: "I am here to tell you that **I am not tired any more.** However, if it was not for my church, I would either be dead or a dying drug addict today!" I believe, as does your hosting church's pastor, that the local church is God's support group. It is designed by God to meet the spiritual needs of all people. When the spiritual needs of people are met, then other needs fall in line and become easier to manage. As a program, we strongly encourage you to visit the church that hosts this meeting for addicted people. Something must be different about this church if they are so willing to have this program for you. Why aren't others?

In conclusion to this chapter, I want you to understand something about this book. It is a progression of truth. What that means is that we will begin to explain things to you about your addiction choice—**PORNOGRAPHY**. We will teach you the mental physical effects of **PORNOGRAPHY**, explain the soulical effects (which are the effects of the addiction to your mind, will, and emotions), and expose the negative spiritual effects.

When we begin to expose the spiritual effects that your wrong behavior has had and will have on your life and your eternity, the truths will begin to progress from simple to understand to quite obscure. You may not quite comprehend everything you read, at least not at first. But, stay with it and gain the information. Your confidence in the truth taught may progress over time, but it is important that we explain it all right away and right here.

The three truths that will be expressed are called **justification**, **sanctification** and **glorification**. Those are Old English words for modern day phenomenons. They are literal experiences that will take place in everyone's life who believes in Jesus. These three experiences are what we want you to understand, as God enables you to, that you may experience a lasting victory.

Most Christian books that are written for first-time church or class visitors only explain how one can get to heaven when they die. But, they often fail to explain how to enjoy the journey there! In these topical books on addiction recovery, Dr. Crabb and I will explain truths that make up what we call the "Hidden Life," which is our life hid IN the Life of Christ (or, HID-IN-Life). We will introduce you to a pilgrimage that will give you lasting victory over your **PORNOGRAPHY** addiction. This pilgrimage of the HID-IN-Life will bring you a peace and joy that you may have thought was not available to the inhabitants of this world.

In conclusion, be excited about this fact. The secret that has remained hidden to you that will grant you lasting sobriety is this: The life you long for is found in a Life that longs to live withIN you!

May God be with you so that you may change . . . *finally*!

Steven Curington
President and Founder
Reformers Unanimous Ministries

Jeremy's Testimony

My name is Jeremy, and I am a 23 year old young man. I want to share with you how I found freedom from a 12 year addiction to pornography. At the age of 12, I had my first exposure to pornography. I was exposed to it by my so-called friends. What started out as something very innocent quickly became a crippling behavior that almost destroyed my life. After I was exposed to pornography, I was instantly hooked. I wanted to get my hands on it as soon as possible. I knew what I was doing was not proper. My parents raised me to know better. I was a straight "A" student all through school and well liked by all my peers and authority. I was a pretty good kid! I never got into much trouble and never did any drugs. I used all this as an excuse to indulge in my behavior. It dwelt in darkness like all destructive behavior does. I thought to myself, "Well, I am a pretty good person. What is wrong with a little indulgence into pornography? After all, it was not hurting anybody." This was a lie, and I bought it hook, line, and sinker.

All the while, my parents did not know what I was doing behind their backs. My destructive behavior stayed pretty well under the radar for most of my adolescent years. When I was a young boy, my father turned away from God due to some major trials in his life. When I was 17, my father got his life right with God. I remember the change in his life, and I was taken back by it. My father was my hero. I had never realized that he had been away from God. I thought of my father as one of the most upstanding men I knew. I also knew that he believed in God. The first time I remember God drawing me to Himself was when my father got his life right with God. Little did I know that over the next year God brought many people into my life that influenced me toward the things of God. My heart was being softened to show me my need for a Savior.

At the age of 18, my dad sat down with me and gave me the gospel message. I heard the gospel message many times throughout my whole life, but I never saw my need. I really did not understand it. I thought I was a Christian because my parents were. I remember when my father gave me the gospel message that night, I felt as if I was standing in a courtroom with "GUILTY" written all over me. For the first time in my life, I saw my need for a Savior. However, the one thought that kept coming to mind was, "If I accept Jesus Christ as my Savior, I cannot continue to indulge in pornography!" Part of me wanted to give it up and part of me wanted to hold on to my pornography. The truth was I liked it. What I did not realize was that Jesus Christ was the only One who could give me a new desire to do right.

In one ear I had the devil saying, "Put this off! You can make a decision for Christ later." In the other ear, I heard Jesus saying, "Come to me for salvation!" There was a great battle for my soul taking place. My dad could see that I was under deep conviction. He said, "If you see your need, you need to make a decision tonight. Do not put it off." I was glad he said that because it shut the devil up for the moment. I called out to Jesus that night and asked Him to save me. I truly believe that Jesus had lived a perfect life, died on the cross for my sin, and rose victorious over the grave on the third day. I knew there was nothing I could do to save myself. I understood that clearly, but what I did not understand was that Jesus was the only One who could give me a power to live a righteous life. The power to overcome pornography would never come from me but from the Lord.

When I accepted Jesus Christ as my Savior, I started to see pornography for what it was – SIN that God hated! I felt so much shame for my sin that I did not want to tell anyone that I had a problem with pornography. After all, I was the person who never did anything wrong, and I had a reputation to protect. I let my pride get in the way, and I truly believe that if I had sought out help from my parents or pastor during the first year of being saved, pornography would have never taken hold of my life like it did. I had a problem, but it did not completely take control of my life. I just assumed I could fight this battle on my own. That is exactly what I tried to do. I was actually able to walk away from pornography for a couple of months, but it was not too long until

I indulged into it again. This began a pattern that would occur over the next several years.

It was at least a year before I said anything to my parents with what I was struggling with. Even when I told them, I was not completely up front with them as to the seriousness of my problem. Little by little they began to realize with horror just how big this problem had become in my life. My parents were shocked to learn how long this had been a part of my life. They were very involved parents, and they did everything in their power to see that I was protected from harm. The only thing that they did not realize was that we had a pipeline of filth being streamed into our home. My parents were naive to how easy internet pornography was to access. By the time I had come to my parents and pastor with my problem, it was already starting to spiral out of control. A lot of heartache could have been avoided had I just opened my mouth in those early days of being a Christian. The next few years would bring great pain to me and those who loved me. Even though I received counsel from my pastor and had tighter accountability from my parents, I found very little victory in my life. I could not go very long without messing up. I was continually up and down. One minute I wanted to serve God with all that was in me, and the next minute I was wallowing in pornography. Each time I looked at pornography, I would tell myself that I would not do it again and that this time would be the last time. My parents and pastor really did not know how to help me. I believed they felt as helpless as I did to fight this addiction. Every time I gave into pornography, it felt like cords binding me tighter and tighter. I felt the grip of the addiction taking hold of me and taking me much farther than I wanted to go.

What started as something very innocent at the age of 12 was now controlling my life and leading me down a path of great destruction. I found myself lying and being very deceitful in order to indulge and going into places I never thought I would go into. I remember looking into the mirror and thinking, "I am turning into a monster!" To the outside world, everything looked fine. Only those who were the closest to me knew of my struggle. In fact, I experienced great success in many areas in my life during that time.

I graduated from college at the top of my class. I started a career as a graphic designer, which had been my dream job for a long time. In many ways, it looked as if I had everything going for me, but I felt that my life was truly falling apart. If there was not a drastic change in my life soon, I knew that everything I worked for would be lost. I was a functioning addict in every sense of the word, but I was ceasing to function. Slowly but surely every area of my life began to be affected. I felt like I was on a roller coaster that did not stop. I became very discouraged and wondered if I would ever be free from this addiction. What was sad was that I did not have anyone standing up to give me much hope. In fact, I was told by good, well-meaning people that I might not get victory in my life and that the Christian life was nothing more than a struggle this side of Heaven. They went on to say that my addiction was just something I would have to deal with, and eventually, with time, things might get better. I had a hard time accepting that! That was not what I found when I read the Bible. But, after about a million times falling, I, too, began to believe the lie that this was just the way it was going to be. I felt utterly and completely defeated!

I remember one day thinking that Heaven would be much better than the hell I was going through here on earth. I had no doubts of my salvation, but I was tired of living defeated. I also did not feel I deserved to live. I felt as if I was doing great harm to the cause of Christ and also to my family with the way my life was going. So, one day I chose to overdose on over-the-counter medication. After doing so, I realized that I did not want to die. I told my mom that I overdosed, and she immediately gave me something to induce vomiting. We did all of this on the way to the emergency room where I found out that my mom's quick action saved my life. I found out from the physician on call that I had indeed taken a lethal amount of medication. By God's mercy my life had been spared. One would think that experience alone would have been enough to turn me around. Not even two weeks later I fell hard. This time, it went to a whole new level. This was the fall that caused me to come to the end of myself.

Four months before all of this, my church started a Reformers Unanimous Program. Reformers Unanimous was the first place that I found hope for the first time. RU was the first place I saw real victory through Christ. I started going to the Friday night classes and began learning what a real walk with Jesus Christ is like. I was no stranger to reading my Bible. In fact, I was very disciplined in reading my Bible. I read it everyday; I read it on the days I fell. I thought if I read my Bible more and did more for God, He would surely give me favor and overcome my addiction. I was very faithful to church as well. I was told that one of the best ways to overcome sin was to just get plugged into church and work hard for God. Well, that worked on the days that I had something to do for the church, but the days that I was not in church, I messed up. I became church dependent. Really, I was trying to depend on my efforts. I thought that all of my service was my walk with God. Through RU, I began to see what a real walk with Christ could be like. But, after my last fall, I knew in my heart that God was leading me to make some drastic changes in my life. Finally, I was completely broken. I no longer trusted myself. I became completely open to whatever God wanted to do in my life. God opened my eyes to the fact that I had been trusting in myself for victory instead of Him. I had no problem accepting the fact that Christ did all the work for salvation, but I felt He expected me to be the one working at changing my life. The Lord opened my eyes to the fact that the same way I got saved was the same way I am supposed to live the Christian life – TOTAL DEPENDENCE ON JESUS CHRIST! This was a major revelation for me that completely changed my life. I soon came to find out that as I developed a dependency on Christ and as God became real to me through His Word, I no longer had an extreme desire to indulge in pornography. God made me free! I had never felt such freedom in my life. Also, during this time, God revealed to me the importance of obeying what He had shown me to be His will. Lack of surrender in the life of a Christian will always lead to failure and powerlessness over sin. When I became open to allowing Jesus to be the Lord of my life, I found what had once seemed impossible to obtain now became effortless in many ways. This was Christ doing the work in me rather than me trying to make it happen myself. The life of Christ in me became a reality for me. I began focusing on yielding to the internal persuasion of the Holy Spirit. God prepares me for my day in the morning, prompting me with Bible verses. As I meditate on the verses throughout the day, the Holy Spirit begins to lead me and guide me with the Word of God. I have begun a true walk with God and everything is changing.

I found out that pornography had been my most glaring sin in my life, but I also had many other areas in my life in which I was defeated. Worry was also a great stronghold for me, and God has begun to give me victory in this area also. The good news is not just that Jesus saves from hell but that He saves from sin – ALL SIN! Liberty that comes from walking in obedience to God's Spirit is absolutely amazing. I now work for RU, the ministry that pointed me to the only truth that makes free. I am enrolled in part-time Bible College and want to serve in the ministry for the rest of my life. I hope that Jesus Christ opens your eyes to the freedom that comes from a personal relationship with Him.

Jeremy could not take the internal pain any longer. He saw no way to escape the pain or sense of hopelessness except through continued use of pornography. Like Jeremy, many people of all ages and walks of life battle with the seemingly undefeatable problem of pornography addiction on a daily basis.

Does the scenario of Jeremy describe you or someone you love? Are you searching for answers? There are millions of people just like you or someone you know who are desperately seeking for their way out. Like Jeremy, many have found that way out. They were introduced to "the Way," the Lord Jesus Christ, and have joined thousands of addicts who have found freedom through this program called **Reformers Unanimous (RU)**. RU directs people to the Truth Who makes free. I speak of the Truth named the Lord Jesus Christ. Many have come to an RU meeting, facing a combination of destructive circumstances. Many have sought help on their own, like Jeremy, without any long-term success. Yet, these same people are transformed as they engage in the RU curriculum and participate in its extremely supportive weekly programs.

Thousands of these individuals are now productive members of society. Collectively, they are a living testimony that there is hope for you or for those whom you love.

Yes, pornography CAN be eliminated from your life. There is hope! There is freedom! And, that is the gospel TRUTH!

CHAPTER THREE
The Topic

For those who view pornography, they know exactly how pornography makes them feel. They also recognize that the feeling it generates each time is fairly consistent. However, very few who indulge in pornography actually knows why it makes them feel this way, much less how it happens.

As with all other addictive drugs, it is amazing to learn how effective they are at masking the real root problem in a person's life. Pornography actually manipulates neurotransmitters in the brain that create a false sense of well being. This sense of pleasure and calmness is, of course, only temporary. As well, it is not reality. However, we have a very great Creator who made our body to secrete these neurotransmitters, and He has ways of doing so without the pain and misery of indulging in pornography.

NEUROTRANSMITTERS AND THEIR ROLES IN THE BODY:
- acetylcholine: stimulates muscles, aids in sleep cycle

- norepinephrine: similar to adrenaline, increases heart rate; helps form memories
- GABA (gamma-aminobutyric acid): prevents anxiety
- glutamate: aids in memory formation
- serotonin: regulates mood and emotion
- endorphin: necessary for pleasure and pain reduction
- dopamine: motivation; pleasure

In this chapter, Dr. George Crabb, a board certified Internal Medicine physician and member of the American Society of Addiction Medicine, will explain to us the ramifications behind this behavior, which is a choice for so many.

Jeremy, who we read about earlier, experienced the effects of the destructive behavior of pornography addiction. To understand the effects of pornography on Jeremy, we shall first look at how it worked on his brain. Pornography has a powerful impact

PORNOGRAPHY FACT
The most debilitating consequence of repeatedly yielding to pornographic temptation and sin is the cycle of sexual addiction it leads to.

on the brain's function. Pornography stimulates a group of chemicals called neurotransmitters. Because of this stimulation, Jeremy enjoyed the effects of this elevation of neurotransmitters in his brain through experiences of euphoria. Neurotransmitters are messengers between different nerve cells in the brain. Pornography, as it is viewed by the individual, increases the amounts of these neurotransmitters released in the brain (specifically dopamine), thus, exciting the nerve endings and sending out even more signals. The main neurotransmitter stimulated by pornography is dopamine. Dopamine is related to the reward system. Dopamine reinforces the feelings achieved during pleasurable experiences, such as laughing, eating, exercising, or work. Pornography directly activates these circuits and helps to essentially condition or stamp in behaviors that are not only necessary for survival but are highly destructive, such as pornography. Jeremy became involved with such destructive, compulsive, male-adaptive behavior because of the effect that the increased surge of dopamine in his brain had on him as a result of his pornography addiction. This led Jeremy, as well as many others, into a life of self destruction.

Pornography may well be the single most insidious element within this country, and the cause of a variable avalanche of problems including:

- Child Molestation
- Incest
- Child Kidnappings
- Mutilations
- Murder
- Every Other Conceivable Type of Sexual Perversion

Pornography is an addiction, and, like any other addiction, it will escalate. You cannot dabble in destructive behavior up to a certain point and then drop it. It continues to escalate until it destroys the person involved. Secular humanists tell us that pornography is no more than a harmless, albeit, colorful quest for pleasure. We are finding out differently, however. With pornography, as with all other addictions, sooner or later the appalling, final consequences will surface. Pornography is not without consequences!

Recent studies in the medical community have demonstrated sinister results connected to pornography. Webster's Dictionary tells us that pornography is the "*depiction of erotic behavior as in pictures or writing intended to cause sexual excitement.*" It involves such materials as books, photographs, television, movies, internet, and the like. All of the above depict erotic behavior and are intended to cause sexual excitement. In my medical opinion, pornography, like any other addiction, falls into **four categories**, and they are absolutely predictable.

1. ADDICTION

Pornography is as addictive as alcohol, drugs, or gambling. Pornography is not something an individual can pick up and lay down or escape at will. It takes but a short time before the individual becomes addicted. Sadly, a high percentage of printed pornography eventually falls into the hands of children.

2. ESCALATION

Addiction takes only a short time and then escalation sets in. "Old pornography" is not as stimulating as "new pornography." There is no thrill in going over what has been previously viewed. An individual hooked on pornography needs a steady diet of bigger and better thrills. How is this provided? It is provided by deeper and deeper excursions into greater and greater perversion. This is escalation. It is easy to picture how the process begins. Once the individual is hooked, he has to have ever-increasing "doses" of pornography, and these must be of a stronger and stronger stimulation to elicit the arousal originally brought about by previous pornography. What happens when pornography of any type is viewed? It has a specific medical effect on the individual. It has been demonstrated that an actual chemical reaction takes place in an individual's brain when he views any type of pornographic material. The chemical reaction mediated by serotonin, dopamine, and epinephrine causes these mental images to be imprinted indelibly upon the brain of the individual. They will subsequently be recalled with clarity and such force that the individual is unable to break the chain of events as he falls deeper and deeper under the influence of these unhealthy stimuli. These chemical reactions also have a resulting effect not only upon the mind but also on the body.

3. DESENSITIZATION

Once the individual indulges in pornography, bondage is sure to follow. He becomes addicted until it becomes something he cannot pick up or put down at will. At this point, it begins to escalate. He must now wallow deeper and deeper into perversion to satisfy the demands of a mind that is rapidly becoming warped by this disease of hell. Material that would have once been repulsive and horribly shocking now becomes acceptable and even commonplace. The man who would not have ever considered molesting a child now starts to "get his kicks" by watching child molestation (or child abuse) on movies or by reading about it. It no longer repulses him. He is almost another person. Incredibly, the hard-core addict can watch a woman being raped and have no normal reaction of revulsion. To the contrary, he becomes aroused and sexually excited by viewing this "ghoulish" scene. What has happened? He has become desensitized. Normal responses have been erased and moral and spiritual disintegration have set in until he is finally in total bondage.

4. THE ACTING OUT

We have addiction followed by escalation and desensitization, and, finally, the acting out of the role. After viewing films, reading such material, viewing it on the Internet, and gradually becoming more and more debased, the individual suddenly finds himself desirous of acting out the role he has been viewing or reading about. At this point, he may try to get his wife or girlfriend to act out the female role in such situations, whatever it may be. If he does not have a wife or girlfriend, prostitution is resorted to with strange women or even children against their wishes. The compulsion does inevitably develop, however, to act out the role.

Ask Jeremy or anyone else who has struggled with an addiction to pornography about the effects. They will, without exception, describe a nightmare.

Friend, regardless of where you may be in your struggle with pornography addiction, the good news is that there is life after pornography. Jeremy found this life. For this to be accomplished in your life, there must be a change in your behavior. I want you to know that the only effective way of changing your behavior is changing the beliefs to which you hold. This will be the subject of the remainder of this book.

When viewing the world of pornography addiction, we often envision a scenario of total victimization. But, the cold reality of pornography addiction is that it is a deliberate, destructive *choice* made by the user that is followed by many similar bad choices. In other words, it is a lifestyle of repetitive, bad choices. Bad choices will be made in nearly every area of a pornographer's life because of this single bad choice to view pornography, even once!

Pornography is a release for the viewer, albeit, temporary. It relieves the pain that dwells in the deepest, darkest dungeon of one's life. A user may be thinking, "It is no big deal!" Choosing to believe that is merely one's attempt to minimize and deflect attention away from their problem. My friend, pornography is a big deal. It is a major issue that affects the body, soul, and spirit of an individual. You may think it is a necessary ingredient for having a good time and getting your work done, but oh how far from the truth is that lie?!

However, if you picked up this book at an RU class or received it in some way from someone who cares about you, then you might by thinking, "I know someone like that!" Or, you may even say, "That's me!"

So, why do you do what you do? The reasons behind your destructive behavior are many. Perhaps the most common reason for viewing pornography is because it is a coping mechanism.

All of us learn to handle stressful and negative events in different ways. We feel "out of control" because of internal pain, frustration, and anxiety. Our natural response is to alleviate the pain. Unfortunately, many people find temporary relief in viewing pornography.

Dr. Crabb is 100 percent correct. If you find yourself living your life this way, then you have developed an unhealthy coping mechanism. A coping mechanism is simply how a person chooses to deal with disappointments. Prior to my role as Reformers Unanimous President and

Founder, I was addicted to powder cocaine and alcohol for over ten years. Whenever I would use cocaine or alcohol, the overwhelming difficulties from which I was running seemed to disappear.

I believe that our many inner hurts is what creates our desire to escape reality. That internal hurt drives one to use drugs, drink alcohol, or view pornography as a way to relieve the pain. But, unfortunately, the pain and hurt is always still there when the drugs, alcohol, or pornography is gone.

As someone who personally knows the bondage of cocaine and alcohol and has found freedom from their gripping control, I want you to know that believing your hard or hurt feelings are best handled with the coping mechanisms of methamphetamine, cocaine, alcohol, another mood altering drug, or viewing pornography is an absolute lie. It is a lie from your spiritual enemy, Satan, who seeks to entrap then destroy you. Our desire is to reveal to you the Truth. If you will choose to reject any lies you have believed and choose to live in this Truth you are learning, then the power the lies possess over you will be broken.

The Bible promises those who Jesus has made free are freed indeed (see John 8:36 at the back of this book for actual Bible wording)!

Pornography is only a temporary fix. It does not remove the pain caused by your unmet needs. It simply temporarily masks it. The condemnation and feelings of guilt and shame that many addicts carry from past failures, abuses, or unhealthy relationships inside and outside the family can lead to a self-hatred deep in their soul for which they desperately desire relief.

You have turned to pornography, choosing it to be your preferred way of dealing with this internal turmoil. This improperly handled internal turmoil eventually leads the user to become depressed. Depression then facilitates viewing more pornography. Always remember this: Depression **can** and usually **will** control your entire life.

Feelings of depression lead a person to feel that they have no control and that things will never change. They feel they are in a deep, dark hole with no legitimate way out. They see the only way out to escape their mental anguish is by viewing pornography.

A pornographer's thinking is all based on a lie. Having accepted this lie, they now have a distorted view of reality. Their whole concept of life has become skewed. How could someone come to believe that something so damaging and destructive, like pornography, can bring relief? The answer is found in this truth: Wrong behavior is *stimulated* by a process of wrong thinking. Wrong thinking is *permeated* by wrong beliefs.

To change our behavior, we must change our thinking. And, to change our thinking, we will need to change a great many of our wrong beliefs about ourselves, God, and even about others. In other words, our beliefs must be dealt with in order to experience eventual, true and lasting freedom.

So, we see that viewing pornography is a vicious cycle with no apparent way out. However, there is a way of escape! I have escaped and am no longer an addict. Jeremy has escaped and gone on to live a successful life, as have I. You have tried to find your own way of escape, haven't you? It has not happened. You have constantly failed. Your failures have only increased your pornography use and its hold on your life, leading to deeper pain. But, the Bible has the answer.

Jesus, whom in John 8:32 tells us is "the Truth," beckons for you to turn to Him. He wants to break the chains that hold you in bondage. He wants to restore and comfort you into a right relationship to God, to others, and even to ourselves.

Dr. Crabb is an expert on addiction recovery. As a member of the American Society of Addiction Medicine, he has partnered with me and our ministry to help everyone understand that the real bondage of addiction is not physical, or even mental. It is spiritual.

The Truth of Jesus and the truths of Jesus will give you a life of joy. Jesus called it an "abundant life." But, how do you find Him? And, how do you find the submission to Him necessary to be made free?

Those are good questions. Allow me to

introduce to you the Answer, Jesus Christ. He is the answer that Jeremy and I have found in our quest to be cured of our cocaine and pornography addiction. Jesus is the only One who can touch your heart so deeply that your life can literally change forever.

Our media tends to portray Christians in a very unattractive way. They even like to make them look stupid or "extra dependant" on a crutch of some sort to get through life. I've heard it said on national television by a well known actor that "Christians are weak people who can't stand the thought that they only have one life, so live it up! They just gotta' believe in giving this life up for some hope of another world that doesn't exist!"

Can I ask a question? How would a Hollywood actor know if there is another world? And, if he is wrong and I am right, how sorry would he be that he was on the wrong end of that opinion.

It is sad that Christians are portrayed on television and in movies as idiots because this portrayal has a profound impact on those who are so gullible to society's ways of manipulation. The truth is that very smart people, many presidents, kings, mega large corporate CEO's, and millions of others profess themselves to be believers in Jesus Christ as their only way to Heaven. Are they stupid, gullible, or in need of some crutch? I would say not.

As a matter of fact, you know what? They are happy people! A great many of them live victorious lives over vice. It is almost unheard of for a Christian to commit suicide. There must be a reason why so many rich or famous people who do not possess Christ profess such misery in life. They are unable to find any satisfaction though they have tried and tried and tried.

Yes, the world is influenced by Hollywood actors, media moguls and personalities, millions of other CEO's who are miserable; but there are even more engineers, machinists, construction workers, secretaries, wait-staff, and busy mothers who do not know this Christ of whom I speak. Glaringly, you can see their lifestyle bound to selfish pride, ingratitude, depression, and many other debilitating behaviors.

I think it is easier to believe in a Creator that put you here for a reason and wants you to be at peace with Him and to fulfill that reason for your existence than it is to believe, "We only live once—enjoy it!" Boy, I would hate to be wrong on that decision and live eternity in hell because I would rather continue in wrong and never be forgiven for it.

Jesus came to make us free. He will make you free from guilt, shame, condemnation, and hatred. He will make you free to enjoy a life of peace, joy, satisfaction, and among other things, sobriety. Jesus will illuminate the root causes of your addiction. Not only will He show you the problem, He will show you the answer to your problem. Jesus will never harm, hurt, or betray you. The love Jesus has for you will never change because His love is not based on you or your performance, but solely based on His character, which never, ever changes.

The Bible tells us that, to conform our lives to something worthwhile and fulfilling, we must transform the way that we think. (See Romans 12:2 in the back of this book.) Transformation is the word *metamorphosis*. It means "to change in form." In this case, we want to change our forms of thinking. The best way to change our way of thinking is not to "try" to think differently, but rather to first change the way we believe. When our beliefs change, then so can our thoughts.

For example, you remember the super hero the Incredible Hulk? Whenever his alter ego, David Bruce Banner, became angry or outraged, a startling "metamorphosis" occurred. He went from being calm, cool, and collected to a raging monster because he struggled to handle adversity. Anger was a trigger that changed this otherwise calmed man into the form of a monster. That was a negative and dangerous transformation.

However, there was another super hero that was far more "mild mannered." I am speaking of Clark Kent. Clark Kent never broke a sweat when faced with adversity. How could he stay so calm, so cool, and so collected no matter the level of threat he faced? It was because he knew he had a power living within him that gave him supernatural abilities. Clark Kent, remembering this during extremely difficult times, made it possible for himself to "transform" into a dependable person in times of trouble.

Well, that is the transformation we all need! And, that, my friend, is the transformation that RU wants you to experience. Not a transformation in which you become a super hero, but one in whom you become Supernatural.

There are three benefits of salvation (accepting the truth…JESUS): justification, sanctification, and glorification. It is these benefits that grant us not only the freedom from sin's *penalty*, but also the freedom from sin's *power*, and eventual freedom from sins' *presence*.

In our next chapter, we will explain to you how to have your payment for your sin debt (death and hell) paid by the One who died for all. We want everyone who attends our classes to clearly understand how they can accept Jesus Christ, the Truth, as their personal Savior. We will do this here for you by explaining to you God's Simple Plan of Justification. It comes from a complete transformation.

CHAPTER FIVE
Our Transformation Through Justification

Now, I understand that the purchase of this book indicates that you or someone you love struggles with **PORNOGRAPHY.** And you probably were not necessarily interested in finding religion; you want to find **FREEDOM!** But, my friend, there is no freedom without the Son of God. If you want to be freed, you will have to go through the only Way that grants freedom. You gain freedom through the sacrifices made on our behalf by Jesus Christ.

Jesus wants to help you! He has already provided a way of escape for you. Choosing to continue in your addiction to pornography is, in essence, denying and rejecting the freedom Jesus offers to you. Trying to construct your own answers to your addiction or even your other problems in life is like saying that the torture Jesus went through for you on the cross was not enough. He would need to do more for you to turn to Him.

No! His death was enough to pay not only the penalty for your sin, but also to provide you with the emancipation from the power of your sin,

as well. Yes, true freedom begins by accepting Jesus Christ's substitutionary death on the cross as your penalty payment for all the wrong you have ever committed. All of it, one payment. God's sinless Son died for you. We refer to this as "accepting Christ as your Savior."

If you have never done this in your life, there is no other step, much less twelve steps you can take to find freedom. This is a "change in belief" that each individual must make for themselves. It is the most important choice you will ever make.

Justification is a benefit that takes place at the moment of salvation. Justification is salvation from the *penalty* of sin (which is the Bible word for our wrongs). The penalty from which we are being justified is the penalty of eternal separation from God in a place called Hell.

To help you picture what Christ has done for you and me, there are some key words in the Bible I want to help you understand. What Jesus Christ actually did **for us** needs to be understood before we can clearly accept His gift and establish the pathway to freedom from our addictive nature.

Sin is the Bible word for our wrong. The Bible tells us that everyone does things wrong and everyone does wrong things. This makes us sinners. (See Romans 3:23)

Our wrongs must be paid for in some way and someday. It is a huge debt! The Bible tells us the payment for our wrong doing is death. (See Romans 6:23)

We are all sinners and so are you. Your drug of choice is just one of the many sin problems that you have. You may think the best choice you could make is avoid viewing pornography. But, the worst choice you can make is to die as an unconverted sinner. You will spend eternity in hell.

Do you really believe that you are a sinner? As you enter our program, ask yourself this question. "Do I realize I am a sinner, and that my sin deems me worthy of hell?" If you do not know this, your beliefs must change, my friend, if you are going to be made free in life.

Step One: Accept the fact that you are a sinner. Express to God in dependence upon Him your agreement with the Bible that you are indeed a wrong doer, a sinner!

DEATH

Death means to be absent of life. The Bible tells us that because of sin, God determined that man would become mortal. As a result of that decision, eventually each person physically dies because of our wrong doing. (See Romans 5:12)

However, if we die in our sins, we are destined for hell and separated from God for eternity. Hell is God's judgment and final rejection of the lost. But, it is not a rejection because of our imperfection; it is judgment for our rejection! God loves us, even as sinners, but our sin exempts us from our ability to enjoy Heaven (for those who do not accept His free gift of Salvation).

That free gift was borne by God's Son, Jesus, who willingly offered His own life as a substitute to pay for our debt. Jesus paid our sin debt when He willingly submitted to die for us by being crucified on the cross. (See Romans 5:8)

Do you believe that Jesus died for you and me? If not, please remember that our beliefs must change, my friend, if we are going to be made free in life. Please don't die refusing to believe that you are a sinner and that Jesus died for you.

Step Two: As you continue your prayer from step one, agree with the Bible through your own personal dependence that Jesus died for your sins.

The Bible tells us that after Jesus died, His followers borrowed the tomb of a wealthy believer and laid Jesus' body to rest in that tomb. It was guarded every hour of the day by Roman soldiers. (See Matthew 27:62-65) After three whole days, some close friends of Jesus came to visit the tomb, and found it empty! The body of Jesus was missing! Some thought He had been stolen. But, the Bible says that an angel of the Lord was sitting nearby and informed Jesus' friends that He was gone, for He had risen from the dead. (See Matthew 28:5-7)

Do you believe that Jesus was buried for you? If not, please remember that our beliefs must change, my friend, if we are going to be made free in life. Please don't die refusing to believe that you are a sinner and that Jesus died and was buried for you.

Step Three: As you continue your prayer from step two, agree with the Bible through your own personal dependence that Jesus was buried and laid in state for three whole days.

RESURRECTION

Resurrection means "brought back to life." The Bible tells us that God the Father raised Jesus, His Son, from the dead through the power of His Holy Spirit. (See First Peter 3:18.) Yes, after being crucified and lying in a tomb for three days, Jesus came out of the grave alive! Hundreds of eye witnesses saw Him, proving that this phenomenon is truth.

You see, God is love. God loved us so much that He sent His Son to die for us (See John 3:16.), and He loved His Son so much that He raised Him from the dead. You see, death's power over us would not have been conquered unless God could demonstrate His power over it. Thus, the resurrection of Jesus is important to understanding what He has done for us. Yes, God has power over life, and He has power over death. He can give us the *promise* of His life, and He can save us from our *penalty* of our death.

Do you believe that Jesus was resurrected from the dead by God through the power of His Holy Spirit? If not, please remember that our beliefs must change, my friend, if we are going to be made free in life. Please don't die refusing to believe that you are a sinner, that Jesus died, was buried, and rose from the dead the third day.

Step Four: As you continue your prayer from step three, agree with the Bible through your own personal dependence that you believe that Jesus rose from the dead after three days, by the empowering Holy Spirit.

These three simple words—death, burial, and resurrection—are three words that represent the miracle events that provide us freedom from the penalty of our sins. Receiving this payment frees us from paying the debt for our sin. If you have accepted this gift, then according to the Bible, you now have a home in heaven reserved for you. We do not get to heaven based on what we have done, but by believing in what Christ has done *for* us. We have to believe by dependence on the events described in these three words in order to be saved from Hell and granted a home in Heaven.

That brings us to our final two important word definitions. Those final two words are "believe" and "receive." After this, we will focus on how depending on the events that surround these single word meanings will also help YOU overcome your addiction to pornography. These simple words, their meanings and the events we are defining will provide you, as it has us, a great peace that simple sobriety could never afford!

BELIEVE

The word **believe** means, "to be persuaded to accept a truth through complete dependency upon it." The Bible tells us that Jesus is the Truth and anyone who knows this Truth will be made free. (See John 14:6 and John 8:32)

However, in order for Jesus' sacrifice to be applied to our personal sin debt, we must "be persuaded to accept this Truth of Jesus' death, burial, and resurrection through complete dependency upon it." When we are fully persuaded that something is true, we will depend upon that truth, that is to say, we will believe it!

Belief is another word for confidence or faith. But, your confidence in something must be accepted through a **complete dependence** upon the truth believed in order to qualify as real faith. In other words, in order to be saved, you must "completely depend on Jesus" as the payer of your sin debt through His DBR (death, burial, resurrection). We must have confidence in Him that leads us to depend on Him alone to save us from the debt we owe for our wrong doings in life.

With that said, we do not *need* to add good works, or join a church, or give money, or even "go to confession" to get to Heaven. We only depend on His DBR! That is what the Bible calls "saving faith." We must **believe** *on* Him in order to **receive** Him. Now, what do we receive when we believe on Him?

RECEIVE

Receive means "to obtain from another." The Bible tells us that if we will believe in our hearts that Jesus died on the cross and that God raised Him from the dead that we would be saved. (See Romans 10:9) When we are saved, our sin debt is paid and He gives to us eternal life. If you believe on Him, you will receive this from Him.

Eternal life is best defined as "life in perpetuity." This is to say, it is a life that begins when we get saved (or, are born again) and lasts forever. That is why we can commit to you that your new life will provide you power over your PORNOGRAPHY addiction. It has for me and many others just like me.

Our eternal life cannot be taken from us. (See 1 John 5:1) It is a free gift that cannot be earned by doing good or be taken away by doing bad. It is yours, if you will only believe and receive. Should we? Oh, yes, we all should. Could we? Oh yes, we all could accept this free gift. But, would you? That is the most important question that you will ever answer.

Salvation also gives us the empowering of Internal Persuasion. When we receive Christ as our Savior, the Bible tells us that His Holy Spirit comes to live within us. (See Ezekiel 36:27.) He lives within our spirit in what the Bible calls our inner man. Within the inner man, your spirit and the Spirit of God can have fellowship one with another. This is where we find our ability to worship God and the ability to gain victory over our vices, including, of course, PORNOGRAPHY!

This is God's simple plan of salvation, benefit number one—justification. When we experience justification, we **have been saved** from the *penalty* of sin.

Would you like to believe and accept Jesus Christ as your Savior? It is the first step to freedom from the power of sin, but it is the most important step. This is the step that grants us the freedom we all need from the *penalty* of sin. As a matter of fact, if you find escape from PORNOGRAPHY and other life crippling addictions but die and go to hell, your sobriety will not have been worth it whatsoever.

Friend, I plead with you today to take this first

step! Consider praying this simple prayer to God, meaning it from your heart. Saying this prayer is a way to declare to God that you are depending on Jesus Christ alone for your salvation. The words themselves will not save you. Only dependence (faith) on Jesus Christ can grant us our salvation!

PRAYER: "Father, I know that I am a sinner and my sins have separated me from you. I am truly wrong and deserve to be punished for it. But, do believe that your Son, Jesus Christ, died to pay my sin penalty. I believe that He was buried for three days and was resurrected from the dead by the power of the Holy Spirit. I believe Jesus is alive, and hears my prayers. I accept His payment for my sins and invite His Spirit to indwell me and empower me to overcome my wrong behaviors. In Jesus' Name I pray, Amen."

If you have prayed this prayer, you need to let another Christian know as soon as possible. Contact your RU leader, your RU director, the church pastor, or another Christian friend so that they can help you fully understand each part of this decision.

Your belief systems are changing, and if you have placed your full dependence upon Jesus to save you, you now have a Presence living within you that can give you the power to behave differently.

In other words, now that you have changed just one of the ways you believed, you are now empowered to change the way you think. This simple step can forever change the way you act.

To overcome the world's many vices, this new relationship you have established with Jesus needs to be developed. This relationship is strengthened by the Power of the indwelling Holy Spirit. The more you know Jesus, not *about* Him, but the more you personally *know* Him, the more *freedom* you will experience over the wrong doings of which you have been forgiven. This personal relationship will set you, as it has us, on a pilgrimage toward the second benefit of your salvation, your sanctification.

CHAPTER SIX
Our Conformation Through Sanctification

After we have experienced the transformation of justification, we can soon see a developing **Power source within us that gives us the ability to behave differently.** This Power source is the indwelling Holy Spirit of God. He is real, though it may seem spooky when defined. His Spirit gives us the ability to do things we would never be able to do in our own power. Not just overcoming our addictions, but living a life that is pleasing to God and man, loving your family and others, serving unselfishly and becoming a person who gives of oneself to meet the needs of others. These are just some of the great things that will be produced when you conform into the image of God.

The word **conform** means "to be poured into a mold." The world naturally pours its inhabitants into a mold. At this stage of your life, you are conformed to this world's belief system, which, by the way, got you in the trouble you are in. But, the Bible tells us that God does not want us conformed to this world, but rather He wants us conformed

> "BEING RAISED AS A PASTOR'S KID, I WAS INSTRUCTED IN BIBLE KNOWLEDGE. BUT, I HAD TO CHOOSE, AS YOU DO, TO TAKE THAT KNOWLEDGE AND BEGIN TO KNOW JESUS IN A DYNAMIC, INTIMATE RELATIONSHIP." —DR. GEORGE CRABB

to the image of His Son Jesus Christ. (See Romans 12:2.) This takes place through a process that the Bible calls sanctification. Sanctification is the process whereby we actually develop a personal relationship with Jesus Christ, using the communication Tool of the indwelling Holy Spirit of God. At RU, we will help you understand not only the importance of this relationship, but also the simplicity of a dynamic love relationship with Jesus. At RU, our entire curriculum is designed to help you develop this relationship called sanctification.

Sanctification is the second of our three benefits in God's plan of salvation. Like justification, this takes place the moment we accept Jesus as our personal Savior. *Sanctification* means "to be set apart for sacred use." However, just because we are set apart for sacred use, does not mean that

God is using all believers sacredly!

Many believers fail to disciple, or become students of Christ's. If we do not become students of Christ as disciples, we will never learn about Him. The information we will fail to gain will make it difficult for us to develop a relationship with Him. If we fail to enjoy the benefits of our sanctification, we will seldom enjoy the power of God on our lives!

Failing to develop a walk with Christ is the wrong way for a believer to live their new Christian life. If you make this mistake too, you will fail to overcome many different sins in your life, especially the **PORNOGRAPHY** addiction that brought you to our program.

At Reformers Unanimous, our program focus is on developing our students to enjoy the benefits of their sanctification. Our students consist of newborn believers and long-time believers that are discouraged and apathetic Christians. We help these students obtain their walk with God through our intense discipleship curriculum, effective and motivational classes, individual, personal and group counseling, navigational principles that lead to prosperity in life, and active participation in church related events. All of the personal development we invest in the students of RU is free of charge. The only charge at RU is for cost of the books you may *choose* to purchase.

During our class time, we are instructed to develop as our goals the following eight "ships" as our system for overcoming the power that our addictions have gained over us:

Worship—humbling oneself in order to exalt God in personal praise.

Discipleship—learning how God acts, how man acts, and how man acts when he is trying to act like God in his own power.

Relationship—developing intimacy through a daily *talk* with God that produces a day-long *walk* with God.

Fellowship—an association between people of like faith that we may enjoy the stability that comes from accountability.

Followship—placing our life's most important decisions and choices under the influence of our God-ordained leadership, our umbrella of protection.

Leadership—placing our time and talents under the jurisdictional oversight of our God-ordained leaders.

Stewardship—placing our tithe (to be explained later) where God demands and our treasures where God directs.

Apprenticeship—learning from a personal Spirit-filled trainer how to love God, love others, and to serve God and others out of an appreciation for that great love.

Each of these "ships" are developmental stages. They are detailed in the Reformers Unanimous book, <u>Eight Ships That Shape Your Ship—Shipshape!</u> You can order this important book and many other RU materials at your chapter book table, church bookstore or online at **www.reformu.com**.

In this small, spiritual booklet on PORNOGRAPHY addiction, it would be difficult to explain all that a believer needs to understand concerning the sanctification process. However, we will attempt to explain sanctification in this chapter as an overview of its many benefits to your new-found faith.

Please remember that sanctification is a lifelong process of aligning every part of your soul and body with the indwelling Spirit of the living God. This DOES NOT take incredible work on our part. Rather, it takes an intimate walk where you and He seldom part!! This walk with the Christ that saved our soul will grant us the Power over any bad habit, including PORNOGRAPHY.

You see, when we first began to dabble with sinful vices, they did not bind us. They seldom even restricted us. They were enjoyable and satisfying in the many ways listed in chapter three. But, over the course of time, it began the process of becoming a stubborn habit. That stubborn habit is now a full-fledged addiction that is in the process of taking your whole world away from you. It was a four step process that placed you in this position.

Your addiction began as a **TOEHOLD**. As a toehold, it was a bit of an inconvenience at times, but did not really slow you down too much. The enjoyment was worth the nagging sensation you often felt the next day. However, as you fed that appetite, it only grew stronger. An appetite once fed never grows weaker. It only grows stronger.

Eventually this habit grew to be a **FOOTHOLD**. As a foothold, it slowed your progress. You didn't seem to advance as quickly or recover as fast from the mistakes this habit was causing you to make.

However, you still advanced, albeit awkwardly, and you still recovered. But, eventually, your foothold became a **STRONGHOLD**. As a stronghold, it has become, well, just that—something that has a strong hold on you. As a stronghold, it not only slows your progress, but it also slows your productivity, like a pair of handcuffs would. You are not as productive in your personal life or your professional life and everything begins to fall apart.

It is at this stage that most of our students reach out to our "out-patient" local church addictions program for help. They are still functioning in society, but barely. They are losing jobs, experiencing failed marriages and their homes are often broken at this stage. It is sad when they are at this point in their life for often they are just beginning to look for help. But, it is a very difficult process to find freedom on your own. I believe it

> "THESE FOUR STAGES ARE ILLUSTRATED AS AN "INFECTIOUS" PROCESS. A SKIN INFECTION STARTS AS A MICROSCOPIC INVASION, THEN SPREADS TO SURROUNDING SKIN, THEN INTO THE DEEPER TISSUE, AND FINALLY INFILTRATES INTO THE BLOOD SYSTEM WHERE IT CAN NOW DESTROY THE WHOLE BODY."
> —DR. GEORGE CRABB

is nearly impossible. Without Jesus you may find sobriety, but you will not find contentment in the difficult journey of life.

However, some reject the solutions that many programs offer them and carry on with their addictive habits until the addiction develops from a stronghold into a full blown **STRANGLEHOLD**. A stranglehold will takes us wherever it wants us to go and restricts us from going anywhere we may want to go. Though a stronghold will bind you, a stranglehold will enslave you. It will control your entire life's existence. You live to feed it, and if you don't feed it, you will begin to think you are going to die!

At the stranglehold stage, you are a non-functioning addict. At this point, you will probably need a full-time residential program. This is the stage we find most of our applicants to our men's and women's residential Schools of Discipleship homes in Rockford, IL. The folks in our homes are barely functioning and they CANNOT find freedom unless they leave behind their troubled environment.

Our residential Schools of Discipleship (**www.ruhomes.org**) is a program that acts like a green house. It protects an addict from their environment so that they can grow really fast. If this is where you find yourself, please understand that those whose addiction appears to have a stranglehold on them will find great help at RU and the church that hosts it, but it may be necessary to take a break for a period of months in your life and recover from the snare in which you have found yourself.

With these four stages of addiction understood, we can see how sanctification is not the only lifelong process. Your personal destruction has been developing for a great portion of your life, as well. The moment we begin to rebel as young men or women against the authority system that God designed, we began a journey that leads to our eventual ruin. For me, that ruin emanated from addictive, sinful habits that I formed as a young man in rebellion to my parent's wishes.

For most people with addiction problems, it has taken a long time to develop these bad habits. It will take some time as well until your spiritual development will be strong enough to overcome those habits. However, most of our students see great victory almost instantaneously and experience lasting victory shortly thereafter. Why? Because in the process of sanctification, it is God that does the work, not the recovering addict.

With that said, God intends for our recovery process to begin at conversion through the justification of our soul and the sanctification of our spirit. God intends for the benefits of sanctification to begin at our conversion to Christ and to be increasing in enjoyment throughout the remainder of our lifetime. In justification, we are "made right in heaven." Sanctification is how we become "more right on earth."

When we accept by faith God's simple plan of salvation, we are entitled to the benefits of sanctification. The primary benefit of justification is freedom from the *penalty of sin* but the primary benefit of sanctification is freedom from the *power of sin*. The benefits that come from submitting to God's process of sanctification is what leads us to the abundant life that Jesus promised to those who would live their life IN Christ Jesus.

To best explain how sanctification grants us His Power over sin and thus neutralizes the need to overcome sinful addictions in our own power, we will look at the **same six key words** that we defined in our last chapter. Each of these words that we defined in justification will be used to define both sanctification and glorification, as well.

SIN

Do Christians commit sin? The Bible tells us that after we are justified, we are now "made right in heaven". But, that does not make us automatically able to live right on earth. It is not by my power or might that I can avoid sinning, but by His Spirit that I can remain free from the power of sin. (See Zechariah 4:6.)

But, as believers, the issue is no longer whether or not we *commit* sin, but rather whether or not we willingly *permit* sin. (See First John 3:9.) Let me explain what that means. God has given every believer access to His Spirit of Power over the dormant power of sin that remains in our bodies. This wonder-working Power is harnessed within my inner man in the form of God's Holy Spirit. Wrong desires from outside pressure (temptations and trials) after my conversion continue to stimulate my mind to think wrong thoughts. But, it is when my mind chooses to *submit* to that stimulation that I have made the choice to *permit* sin. (See Romans 7:15-17.)

In others words, before we ever *do* wrong, we FIRST choose to *think* wrong! Thus, we do wrong before we actually *did* wrong, if you know what I mean. So, you can see that as Christians, it is not so much that we are sin *committers*. It is that we are choosing first to be sin *permitters*!

The Bible clearly teaches us that if we will not *permit* sin to enter into our thought processes, we will not *commit* those sins. Thus, the Power of God's Spirit is necessary to keep those thoughts from becoming constant daily meditations. (See Proverbs 23:7a.) If we think them, we will enter into unnecessary temptations that, if not handled properly, will lead us back to our addictive, sinful habits.

DEATH

Thinking wrong is a weakness of both the saved and the lost. But, it is the saved who have been given a guaranteed way of escape WITH the bad thoughts. (See First Corinthians 10:13.) Whenever outside pressure (oppression) stimulates our mind to think wrong, a discipled and developed Internal Presence from God will influence us to reject that outside pressure to sin. This "way of escape" will be provided WITH the temptation. Thus, at the same time we are tempted to think wrong, there is an exit ramp in our mind to get off the "road to eventual ruin." If we reject His "way of escape," we will pass by it and be forced to deal with the temptation in our own power. That is to say, we will have to find our own way of escape. Only our strong character can help us at this stage. And, if our will power is weak, we will probably soon commit that sin in our body, for we have permitted that sin to dwell in our mind. (See James 1:14-15)

In order to take the "way of escape" that the Power of His Presence provides, we must be willing to experience a death to self at the moment of His prompting in order to exit this road of ruin. We must literally be willing to **die to self** every day, and throughout the day. To die to self means to reject our selfish desires to think wrong.

So, we see that even as Christ died for us, we must also now be willing to **die *with* Christ**. (See Romans 6:6)

At Reformers Unanimous, our discipleship curriculum will teach you how you may experience that daily death that is a prerequisite for obtaining what the Bible calls the "Power of His resurrection." His Power can work through the life of a flawed man, but His Power works best through the life of a dead man! That is to say, a man that dies to his own selfishness.

BURIAL

When we die to self out of an unselfish desire to obey His promptings, we will experience a satisfaction of sorts. For we learn that when we suffer loss that we enjoy closer fellowship with Him. (See Philippians 3:8 and 10.) This period of intimate "fellowship of His suffering" represents our time of burial. Metaphorically, as we wait for God to empower us to get through a difficult situation, we are in a dormant position. We are dead to our own wishes but not yet alive in His Power. At this time, we are metaphorically secluded from the outside world and its ways, but we have a work going on with Christ in the darkness of our inner man.

This process, which I call our "time in the tomb" precedes the power that comes from His resurrected Life living through us. You may not understand this right now or quite see the symbolism of what I am teaching you, but as you grow and mature IN Christ through our addictions program, these truths will become real and personal to you.

So, we see that the Bible tells us that we are not only crucified *with* Christ as we die to self, but that we are also buried *with* Christ as He destroys the influences that want to control us. (See Romans 6:4) This time of waiting for His power is designed to be a sweet time of rest. But, for many believers, it is rejected and becomes, instead, a time of turbulent wrest.

At Reformers Unanimous, we will teach you through our discipleship curriculum how to patiently wait in your proverbial tomb as that which is "on your mind" may be starved of thought and eventually dissolve from your heart's meditation. When that wrong thought is no longer actively at work in your meditation, the enemy can no longer use it as a tool of manipulation. This allows you to experience the transformation process that grants you the Christ life that comes from His resurrection.

RESURRECTION

Sometimes we circumvent the resurrection process of the Christ Life when we choose to wrest *with* Christ rather than rest *in* Christ. We wrestle *with* Christ when, after we willingly die to self, but because of a difficult circumstance, we impatiently reject our time of waiting in the tomb for His power to come upon us. We, thus, yield to our own devices in order to overcome life's troubles. (See Proverbs 14:12)

We have died WITH Christ. We are buried WITH Christ and He intends for us to patiently await His timetable in order for us to be risen WITH Christ. (See Romans 6:4-5)

At Reformers Unanimous, we will teach you through our training and discipleship curriculum how to patiently wait on the Lord to renew your strength. This process of waiting on Him will surely give us the power that RU promises is available to us to overcome our stubborn habits and addictions. This is a truth you must believe if you are going to see any lasting change take place IN you.

BELIEVE

It takes belief, that is to say, faith, to save us.

But, it also takes faith to change us. Before we are saved, we have very little faith. After we are saved, we are given the "faith of Christ" as one of the nine Fruit of the Holy Spirit. (See Galatians 5:22)

The term "Hidden life" is the daily death from our own affections and lusts in order to experience the Spirit Life. The Spirit Life comes from patiently resting in state for His Power to perform a good work in us. It is when we are "Hid-IN-Life."

To engage in this Hidden Life, we must exercise more dependence on Him than what it took to save us. But, this is not an increased dependence that is quantitive. For dependence is dependence. But, rather, it is an increased dependence that is durative. The duration (or length) of our faith is longer and longer between our "bouts with doubt." This increase of duration in our trust IN Him takes place as we spiritually develop. But, it is not *our* faith in which we are learning to remain confident. It is *His* faith that I must submit myself unto in order to experience the benefits of my sanctification. It takes my faith IN Christ to save me, but it takes *the* faith OF Christ to change me. (See Galatians 2:20 and Philippians 3:9.)

At Reformers Unanimous, our goal is to develop you out of your unbelief. There are many things that our human minds do not immediately comprehend. But, His faith that dwells within our spirit must operate independent of our feelings which dwell within our soul. When we know that God says something is true, we must accept it with the faith that He has placed within us. We cannot do this without a relationship IN Him. At RU, our discipleship curriculum will help you develop that intimate and abiding love relationship with Jesus Christ. If you will believe *in* Him, you receive *from* Him.

RECEIVE

Jesus said that He came that we might have life, and that we might have it more abundantly. (See John 10:10) When we refuse to die *with* Christ, or to lie *with* Christ, or to rise *with* Christ, then our Christian life will be up and down, at best. That is not the *abundant* life; that is the *redundant* life. I want to receive what God has given unto me—eternal life. That life begins at conversion.

But, in order to enjoy eternal life before I get to heaven, I must be willing to *do* as Christ *did*. Die, be buried, and be raised to walk in newness of life. (See Romans 6:4) If I yield to His faith in me, then I will receive His life living through me.

When we receive Christ as our Savior, the Holy Spirit will begin to persuade us through intuition, conviction, and worship. Whenever we reject any aspect of our selfless death, patient burial, and empowered resurrection, we stunt that internal persuasion and hinder our ability to live holy (soberly, righteously, and godly) in this present world. (See Titus 2:12) This will not separate us from God's presence, but it will strain His persuasion over us. We remain sanctified (set apart), but we no longer enjoy the benefits of our sanctification—abundant life, free from the power of sin and addiction.

At Reformers Unanimous, we *do not* help **addicts** live free from sin and addiction. We help **Christians** free live from sin and addiction. If you are a Christian, we believe this program can be a great help to you.

However, for RU to be of service to anyone, one must be willing to continue in this lifelong process of changing the way that we think. At RU, our goal is to help us overcome our "stinkin' thinking" by teaching everyone the biblical way to "tinker with your thinker."

At RU, we want to walk *with* you in our pilgrimage through sanctification. Together we will spiritually develop so that we may overcome all our crippling and habitual sins. Doing so brings us to our final chapter and benefit of salvation— glorification.

With our justification, we have BEEN saved from the PENALTY of sin. With our sanctification, we are BEING saved from the POWER of sin. Our third benefit is the future benefit of glorification. In glorification we shall BE saved from the PRESENCE of sin.

CHAPTER SEVEN
Our Reformation Through Glorification

This final benefit of glorification is the potential to glorify God in this life and the privilege to be glorified by God in the life hereafter. Our chapter title explains that we will be "reformed' thru glorification. Reformed is a key word at Reformers Unanimous, for it makes up the first word in our program's name.

Webster's dictionary defines the word *reform* to mean "to change from worse to better; to bring from a bad to a good state; to improve corrupt manners or morals, to remove that which is bad or corrupt; as, to reform abuses and to reform from vices."

That is a long definition that teaches us what God intends to do in our life. At RU, we hope to assist you in that process whereby God will "change you in more ways than just one." RU does not only focus on developing you from a drug addict to a sober living citizen, though we will focus on your recovery.

At RU, we want to help you experience much

more change than that! We want to see you go from being unsaved to saved. We want you to go from headed to Hell to being Heaven-bound! We want you to go from being a self-focused person to a person focused on others. Yes, and we want you to go from being a bad person to a good person.

This is a process whereby we focus on our spiritual development as well as our personal development. The process of spiritual development has been explained in the previous two chapters of this book. It will also be taught more thoroughly as you engage in our Strongholds Discipleship Program curriculum. In this chapter however, we want to discuss the level of personal development that should follow your Strongholds Course work. This graduate's course work at RU is entitled, "Gaining Remaining Fruit." It is a focus on developing any missing character qualities you may not have in your life. Character qualities are necessary building blocks that God intends for us to learn as children. But, for some people, they fail to have them taught or they have rejected them till much later in life. We want to help you "reform" your character, where needed, from bad to good.

The second word in our program name is "unanimous." The word *unanimous* means "being of one mind." What that means is that at RU we are all unanimously focused on one thing—change! But, it is not a change that is acquired in our own effort, but it is a change that is granted to us by God, through His Spirit for Jesus' sake. We all strive for the mind of Christ. It is this mind that should be within us all. (See Philippians 2:5)

This change requires only one thing from us—a two-fold belief. A confession that believes *on* Jesus through His blood for our justification to save us and a conviction to believe *in* Jesus through His Spirit for our sanctification to change us. When we accept these commitments and believe with all our heart, lasting change is the natural result. That is when the glorification of God begins.

The word *glory* means to "bring the right opinion of." It literally means to "make God look good." The day will come when we will be saved not only from the penalty of sin (our justification), not only from the power of sin (our sanctification), but also from the presence of sin (our glorification). Until the day we enter

Heaven's gate, our focus should not be on OUR glorification but rather on HIS glorification!

The Bible tells us that everything God created was intended to bring Him glory, to make Him look good. That is not the goal of many people's lives today, but God wants that to be our goal. We should strive to meet that goal by trusting in Him to reform us into God-glorifying new creatures in Christ.

With that said, sanctification is the key to glorification. If you are developing a dynamic love relationship with Jesus Christ, you will glorify God in your life. However, there will be times when your walk is weak or the adversity is particularly strong. We like to say at RU that "new levels bring new devils." At times like this, if we don't have strong character to lean on in spiritually weak times, we will be tempted to do things that may eventually lead us back to our addictive behavior. We may not "use" right away, but if we are not quick to make it right with God, we may grow farther from Him and engage in our sins of choice shortly thereafter.

During this process, which is called spiritual

backsliding, we will need to have developed some character if we are going to remain *doing* right as we strive to *get* right. Now, please be advised that strong character is no substitute for strong Christianity. But, without strong character, we will be powerless when God's power is not granted to us.

Most addicts have character in some areas, but lack character in other areas. For example, you may have strong character traits like punctuality, initiative, good work ethic, or attentiveness. But, you may struggle in other areas like rebellion to authority, selfishness, pride, laziness, or jealousy. You can't glorify God especially during difficult times in your life if your weak character fails to improve. Your frustrations will overwhelm you and you will not do right unless circumstances change.

God may not want your circumstances to change. In Christ, you don't have to do right, you just have to submit to desiring to do right, then He does the work for you. However, if we are not abiding IN Christ, we are not right with God. It takes character to *do* right when you are not right.

At times like this, you are the one doing right. This is not God's choice, but it is better than doing wrong. It won't produce joy, but it will keep you from the consequences of sins done in the body. So, character development is important, especially for those who have very little.

However, the Bible says the Spirit of God WILL "sustain your infirmities." That word **infirmities** means "weaknesses." Our indwelling Spirit is strong enough to help us overcome our character weaknesses, even though we may remain personally insufficient to do so in our own power. At RU, we want you to learn to overcome those personal weaknesses as well as spiritually develop. It is designed for your own personal development.

This effort is made on your part by engaging in our graduate's course curriculum. We have two courses for our students. The entry level course is entitled "Strongholds," which is focused on developing the "fruits of the Spirit," which produces "righteousness." But, the graduate's course is entitled, "Gaining Remaining Fruit," which is focused on developing the "fruits of righteousness," which is godly Christian character. This course is designed to help you determine which missing character qualities might drift you back into your addiction during particularly difficult times in your spiritual pilgrimage.

Again, it is important that you understand that any character qualities we may fail to develop as young people are now of secondary importance to being a good Christian. Many people have good character but they may not be good Christians. We only glorify God when people see the strength of our Spirit, not the strength of our soul. In other words, we cannot exhibit the glorification of God to others without first enjoying the benefits of the sanctification of His Spirit—that is to say the benefits that come from developing an intimate personal relationship with Christ. Those benefits are the fruit (which means, "outcome or result") of the Spirit: love, joy, peace, longsuffering, gentleness, goodness, faith, meekness, and temperance.

So, we see that in order for our life to bring God glory right now, we must first focus on developing ourselves spiritually. Now at the same time, God will work on developing our personal lives to become stronger. This combination will be the best way to *stay* strong lest you *stray* weak!

At RU, we look forward to the opportunity of assisting you to spiritually develop first and foremost, and to personally develop you thereafter. However, someday there will be an even better experience for you my friend; and that is eternal glorification!

Someday all believers will glorify God in EVERYTHING that we do FOREVERMORE! The word *glorification* means almost the same thing as glory, or glorify. It means "to exalt One in honor and esteem." Someday, all believers will be exalted to a position where we will ALWAYS bring God honor and esteem. That day will come upon our physical death or His eminent return to earth in what the Bible calls "the rapture." Your RU leadership can explain what that means to you. It will be the most exciting time of your life, I can promise you that.

To date, all but two people who have gone into Heaven have done so as a result of their own physical death. In other words, they have died and awoken in Heaven, so to speak. When a believer's physical life ends, their body dies and their soul enters into Heaven's abode where they will forever bring Him glory.

When we accept God's simple plan of salvation, He does give us the power we need to glorify Him with our lives. It is even God's purpose for leaving us here for so long after our conversions—that others might see Him IN us and believe on His name. This brings God great glory here on earth.

But, from time to time, our lack of faith during particularly difficult times will lead us into failure in certain areas of our lives. At times like this, we will fail to glorify God. Likewise, we will be a disappointment to ourselves.

You see, the Power we need to glorify God comes from being completely yielded to Him. Remaining completely and unequivocally yielded to God is impossible when sin's presence is still alive in our bodies and actively trying to influence our lives.

However, when we are "lifted up to heaven," we will FINALLY experience freedom from the *presence of sin*. This future benefit grants us the sinless perfection that God originally designed for each of us to enjoy. In order to explain how to glorify God here on earth and how the glorification of God in Heaven actually works, allow me to use the same key words that we explained in our chapters on *Transformation Through Justification* and *Conformation Through Sanctification*.

SIN

When we are glorifying God, it is because sin has no dominion over us at a particular time. Its power has been rendered useless for we have chosen to die to the selfish desires of our soul and to yield to the depth of the personal relationship we have established in Christ through faith.

This means that the grace of God has taken over our life and is giving us the power to cast down the imaginations that usually stimulate us to yield to a particular temptation. This is not a once-for-all experience. When we allow our faith to waver to a form of doubt or blatant unbelief in Him, then our relationship suffers and adversity will be much harder to overcome.

Our improved character may keep us from outwardly sinning or even quickly sinning. But, eventually, if we do no rectify the mistakes we are making in our walk with God, then our character will grow weak. This will leave us vulnerable to the internal sin of wrong thinking. Once again, this wrong thinking is found in the meditations of our heart.

Shortly after our wrong meditations begin we will probably give into this contemplation of temptation. When this happens, we will not glorify God for we are no longer under His power. Thus we cannot maintain a righteous lifestyle. It is impossible to live godly in our own power.

This compromise leads us to *permit* sinful thoughts in our mind to overcome the meditations of our heart. Once we permit ourselves to think about sin with any lengthy duration whatsoever, it will eventually cause us to *commit* that sin in our body. It was earlier explained that, when we permit sin to control our heart, we are already engaging in wrong behavior. Thus we will soon commit that wrong. But, we have already permitted ourselves to *being* wrong before we commit ourselves to *doing* wrong. To "be holy" we must give our minds over to God. To "be unholy" we must give our minds over to the things of this world.

This internal permitting of sin in our mind is what separates us from fellowship with God and hinders the Spirit's ability to glorify God with our life. That is how sin will stunt our ability to glorify God here on earth.

However, when Christ shall come, all believers shall see a change take place "in the air." That change will eradicate our sin nature. This means that when we enter heaven, we will have been forever saved from the *presence* of sin. Once again, this rapture really should be explained to you by your RU leader.

DEATH

There are two types of death that lead to glorification. One type of death glorifies God and the other will bring us glorification. Let's first look at the death that brings glory to God. We have discussed it earlier, as well. It is the death of self. When we commit ourselves to dying to oneself and choose rather to live by the prompting of our indwelling Holy Spirit, we are experiencing the benefits of conforming through our sanctification. Some believers do that often, others sometimes, and some hardly ever. Those who rarely die to self do not bring glory to God. Even when they are able to do right, those who know them best recognize it as a seldom experienced victory and will be skeptical of their good works. This will not glorify God. They know the person well enough to know they cannot maintain the consistency that comes only from dying daily to our own selfish wants.

So, God may receive a small measure of glory, but it soon fades as that person falls back into their fleshly, stubborn ways. This is not the type of occasional dying experience that God wants from us. He wants us to die to self every day, throughout the day.

But, we are unable to do so unless we develop a deep abiding relationship with Jesus Christ that manifests itself in wanting what He wants, thinking like He thinks, and feeling the way He feels. We need to nurture our nature to be more like Christ, not by changing our life but by exchanging our life for His life!

The Bible says that when we are crucified spiritually we are crucified WITH Christ. Though we are still alive physically, it is Him that has come to life spiritually. Thus, it is Christ that is supposed to be living His life within me. The Bible says that Christ living in me is the hope of glory. The word *hope* means "expectation." The only expectation I have for bringing God glory is for Christ to live IN me that I may submit to allowing Him to live FOR me. That is the "hid-in-life" we teach at RU.

To bring God glory, not once for a little while, but regularly for long periods, we need to die to self, as prompted by God. This takes a commitment to following the Spirit's leading while learning how to "walk after the Spirit." This is how we glorify God with our lives. It is the Christ Life being accessed through our own personal death to the self life.

However, if we physically perish before Christ returns, then upon our death, it is our human body that experiences death. If we are believers, as outlined in our chapter on transformation thru justification, our soul will never die. Our soul has been spared its much deserved death as a result of our accepting Christ payment on the cross. (See James 5:20.)

Though our body parts will cease to function and we will be buried as we experience our physical death, the soul is incorruptible, it never dies. Our soul will take on immortality in a perfect state as promised by God in His Word. (See First Corinthians 15:53.)

This death will bring US glorification, which once again, is freedom from the presence of sin. However, after our spiritual daily death or our physical once-in-a-lifetime death, there will be a time of burial.

BURIAL

When we die to our selfish wants and wishes, we will be at a proverbial crossroads. At this stage we can climb off that cross as a dead man and resurrect our lives in our power and begin "trying hard to do better." But, if we do this, we will only fail again and again with no real sign of victory.

Or, we ca

upon us t

at that cr

pressure to

to *be* right

of a weaken

easily overloc

This ought

see evil comin

naive people pa

the error of thei

God with our liv ... ...e willing to die and remain buried until Christ resurrects Himself in us. The Apostle Paul (one of the men that God used to pen the words of the Bible) said he died daily, but he never said he resurrected daily. For it was not him that resurrected but rather it was Him!

RESURRECTION

Though we may wrestle with Christ in our own power and have a tendency during times of weak faith to falter as a result, God is faithful to

more than we can
bornness when being
great conviction or even
arly the chastening of the Lord.
e are more willing to "get it over
die spiritually that we may resurrect
Him. If we take this process through its
pernatural course, then we will patently wait
for His indwelling Spirit to lead us out of our
mistakes. This is our spiritual resurrection. It is
our stubborn soul dying, and our developing
spirit resurrecting and taking its rightful role of
authority over our thoughts, wishes, and wants.

This process brings God *great* glory for at times
like this we are humbling ourselves! Bold humility
(Boldness is faith, and humility is trust in God
rather than oneself) is the key to gaining grace
and mercy in our times of need. (See Hebrews
4:16)

This humbling process will keep us from
returning so quickly to the self reliance that
brings us back to a position of pride. Returning
back to our position of pride is what brings us to
another painful crucifixion. Though a crucifixion

for our wrong wishes brings God glory, nothing glorifies Him more than when our submission to His Spirit reveals to others a desire to abide deeper IN Him.

When we die or Christ returns, we will forever be glorified and free from the presence of sin. God's creation will once again function as He had created it in the beginning. Until that glorious day, we ought always to glorify God and not our own selves. This can only be done as we reject sin's *pressure* in our life and yield to God's *power* over sin's presence. This takes only submission to what we have chosen to believe during difficult circumstances.

BELIEVE

My friend, have you believed that Jesus Christ can transform your life thorough the salvation experience of justification? If so, you are born again and you have BEEN saved from the PENALTY of sin, which is death and Hell.

If you have been saved through the faith found in justification, have you also chosen to begin a relationship with Him in which you are learning to follow His leading? If you are doing so, or are committed to do so, then my friend, you are BEING saved from the POWER of sin.

And, finally, are you committed to having a long-term walk with God by yielding yourself to that developing relationship with God's Son through His Spirit? If you do this with regularity and reject compromise in your thought life, then my friend, you will bring God great glory in this life. You have been reformed by your desires to make Him look good with your life!

Your next and final benefit remains to be seen. It will be the day and time when you and I and Dr. Crabb and many untold others will be glorified. It is at that time we will BE saved from the PRESENCE of sin. Until that day, I ask of God that peace be with you. Not a temporary peace that any program may be able to grant you, but the "Peace that passes understanding". It comes only from God as we enjoy and experience all the benefits of your salvation.

The Transformation of Justification: Have you **been saved** from sin's *penalty*? If not, then you need to be justified. If you have been justified, then you will be **judged as a** child of God and saved from sin's *penalty*.

The Conformation of Sanctification: Are you also **being saved** from sin's *power*? If not, then you need to enjoy the primary benefit that comes from sanctification. It is a deep abiding personal relationship with Him that manifests itself in victory over vice. We will make mistakes and find ourselves being **judged as a son**. However, God will develop us like the loving Father He is to be the son we never thought we could be. This development will save us regularly from sin's *power*.

The Reformation of Glorification: Are you victorious in life, enjoying the abundant Christian life? If so, then you are avoiding the disruption that can be caused by sin's presence in the members of your body. That is to be commended. However, the day will come when we will all be **judged as a servant**. How did we serve others? This will take place after our glorification when we **will be saved** from sin's *presence*.

I know that not all of these truths will be easily

or even immediately understood by all who read this book. Very few will have even heard a great many of the facts found in this book, backed up by the Scriptures found in the back of the book. However, that doesn't matter. If you are willing and wanting to learn more about the Truth, He will be revealed to you at a pace that God feels is appropriate for you.

Right now, you may receive from God what the Bible refers to as the "milk of the Word." But, His Word teaches us that as we use it regularly, we will mature to what the Bible calls "strong meat." The truths taught in this book may start as milk and become quite meaty. Worry not. We at RU are here to help you on this journey. And, when your pilgrimage is over, you will be quite pleased with what God has done for you.

In conclusion, I surely hope you will study this book over and over again. And, if you visited one of our chapters recently, we hope to see you again next week.

Scripture Reference

Proverbs 14:12 *There is a way which seemeth right unto a man, but the end thereof are the ways of death.*

Proverbs 23:7a *For as he thinketh in his heart, so is he.*

Ezekiel 36:27 *And I will put my spirit within you, and cause you to walk in my statutes, and ye shall keep my judgments, and do them.*

Zechariah 4:6 *Then he answered and spake unto me, saying, This is the word of the LORD unto Zerubbabel, saying, Not by might, nor by power, but by my spirit, saith the LORD of hosts.*

Matthew 27:62 *Now the next day, that followed the day of the preparation, the chief priests and Pharisees came together unto Pilate,*

Matthew 27:63 *Saying, Sir, we remember that that deceiver said, while he was yet alive, After three days I will rise again.*

Matthew 27:64 *Command therefore that the sepulchre be made sure until the third day, lest his disciples come by night, and steal him away, and say unto the people, He is risen from the dead: so the last error shall be worse than the first.*

Matthew 27:65 *Pilate said unto them, Ye have a watch: go your way, make it as sure as ye can.*

Matthew 28:5 *And the angel answered and said unto the women, Fear not ye: for I know that ye seek Jesus, which was crucified.*

Matthew 28:6 *He is not here: for he is risen, as he said. Come, see the place where the Lord lay.*

Matthew 28:7 *And go quickly, and tell his disciples that he is risen from the dead; and, behold, he goeth before you into Galilee; there shall ye see him: lo, I have told you.*

John 3:16 *For God so loved the world, that he gave his only begotten Son, that whosoever believeth in him should not perish, but have everlasting life.*

John 8:32 *And ye shall know the truth, and the truth shall make you free.*

John 8:36 *If the Son therefore shall make you free, ye shall be free indeed.*

John 10:10 *The thief cometh not, but for to steal, and to kill, and to destroy: I am come that they might have life, and that they might have it more abundantly.*

John 14:16 *And I will pray the Father, and he shall give you another Comforter, that he may abide with you for ever;*

Romans 3:23 *For all have sinned, and come short of the glory of God;*

Romans 5:8 *But God commendeth his love toward us, in that, while we were yet sinners, Christ died for us.*

Romans 5:12 *Wherefore, as by one man sin entered into the world, and death by sin; and so death passed upon all men, for that all have sinned:*

Romans 6:4 *Therefore we are buried with him by baptism into death: that like as Christ was raised up from the dead by the glory of the Father, even so we also should walk in newness of life.*

Romans 6:5 *For if we have been planted together in the likeness of his death, we shall be also in the likeness of his resurrection:*

Romans 6:6 *Knowing this, that our old man is crucified with him, that the body of sin might be destroyed, that henceforth we should not serve sin.*

Romans 6:23 *For the wages of sin is death; but the gift of God is eternal life through Jesus Christ our Lord.*

Romans 7:15 *For that which I do I allow not: for what I would, that do I not; but what I hate, that do I.*

Romans 7:16 *If then I do that which I would not, I consent unto the law that it is good.*

Romans 7:17 *Now then it is no more I that do it, but sin that dwelleth in me.*

Romans 10:9 *That if thou shalt confess with thy mouth the Lord Jesus, and shalt believe in thine heart that God hath raised him from the dead, thou shalt be saved.*

Romans 12:2 *And be not conformed to this world: but be ye transformed by the renewing of your mind, that ye may prove what is that good, and acceptable, and perfect, will of God.*

1Corinthians 10:13 *There hath no temptation taken you but such as is common to man: but God is faithful, who will not suffer you to be tempted above that ye are able; but will with the temptation also make a way to escape, that ye may be able to bear it.*

1Corinthians 15:53 *For this corruptible must put on incorruption, and this mortal must put on immortality.*

Galatians 2:20 *I am crucified with Christ: nevertheless I live; yet not I, but Christ liveth in me: and the life which I now live in the flesh I live by the faith of the Son of God, who loved me, and gave himself for me.*

Galatians 5:22 *But the fruit of the Spirit is love, joy, peace, longsuffering, gentleness, goodness, faith.*

Philippians 3:8 *Yea doubtless, and I count all things but loss for the excellency of the knowledge of Christ Jesus my Lord: for whom I have suffered the loss of all things, and do count them but dung, that I may win Christ,*

Philippians 3:9 *And be found in him, not having mine own righteousness, which is of the law, but that which is through the faith of Christ, the righteousness which is of God by faith:*

Philippians 3:10 *That I may know him, and the power of his resurrection, and the fellowship of his sufferings, being made conformable unto his death;*

Titus 2:12 *Teaching us that, denying ungodliness and worldly lusts, we should live soberly, righteously, and godly, in this present world;*

Hebrews 4:16 *Let us therefore come boldly unto the throne of grace, that we may obtain mercy, and find grace to help in time of need.*

James 1:14 *But every man is tempted, when he is drawn away of his own lust, and enticed.*

James 1:15 *Then when lust hath conceived, it bringeth forth sin: and sin, when it is finished, bringeth forth death.*

James 5:20 *Let him know, that he which converteth the sinner from the error of his way shall save a soul from death, and shall hide a multitude of sins.*

1 Peter 3:18 *For Christ also hath once suffered for sins, the just for the unjust, that he might bring us to God, being put to death in the flesh, but quickened by the Spirit:*

1 John 3:9 *Whosoever is born of God doth not commit sin; for his seed remaineth in him: and he cannot sin, because he is born of God.*

1 John 5:1 *Whosoever believeth that Jesus is the Christ is born of God: and every one that loveth him that begat loveth him also that is begotten of him.*

Dr. George T. Crabb, D.O.
Certified Internal Medicine Doctor
Member of American Society of Addiction Medicine

Dr. Crabb is a long-standing member of Antioch Baptist Church in Warren, Michigan, where his father is the founder and pastor. He is an ordained minister and holds the office of Chairman of the Deacon Board. Dr. Crabb also teaches an adult Sunday school class and serves as Superintendent of Antioch Baptist Academy.

Dr. George Crabb is board certified in internal medicine. He served at the Physician Medical office in Rochester Hills, Michigan, William Beaumont Hospital, and St. John Oakland Affiliation. He is a member of the American Society of Addiction Medicine.

Steve Curington
President and Founder of
Reformers Unanimous International

Steven Curington is the husband of Lori and the father of their five children: Charity, Chase, Channing, Chance, and Cherish. He is the founder of Reformers Unanimous International, a faith based, local-church discipleship program that ministers to the addicted - both within and without the body of Christ. Mr. Curington travels extensively, presenting the ministry and starting chapters of this fast growing support group and discipleship classes in Bible-preaching churches all over the world. He also holds Regional Training Conferences for churches to meet the needs of the addicted in their communities. He is a popular conference speaker and the host of the new radio broadcast Found and Unbound. More information on Steven Curington's ministries, including Reformers Unanimous, is available at his web site: www.reformu. com. Reformers Unanimous International is headquarted in the historical downtown district of Rockford, Illinois.

More Addiction Recovery Booklets

Cocaine —$4.00 (TRB-001)

Alcohol —$4.00 (TRB-002)

Meth —$4.00 (TRB-003)

Marijuana —$4.00 (TRB-004)

Cutting —$4.00 (TRB-005)

Stimulants —$4.00 (TRB-007)

Tobacco —$4.00 (TRB-008)

Heroin —$4.00 (TRB-009)

Eating Disorders —$4.00 (TRB-010)

Prescription Meds —$4.00 (TRB-011)

Self Harm —$4.00 (TRB-012)

Suicide —$4.00 (TRB-013)

Gambling —$4.00 (TRB-014)

order online *www.reformu.com* or call *815-986-0460*

Home Discipleship Course
 # CE-098 $59.⁰⁰

The home study discipleship course is a complete discipleship program in one package for those struggling with addiction. It includes accountability to a local church, and it is an ideal approach for those who are addicted and not near an RU class. These amazing, scriptural materials have helped tens of thousands experience freedom from every addiction in life.

INCLUDES:

1. The <u>Nevertheless I Live</u> Textbook- Life transforming, biblical truths that are taught at RU every Friday night.

2. The <u>Nevertheless I Live</u> Student Guide- The NIL in outline format for note-taking

3. The Strongholds Study Course- A four-part, six-month, in-depth discipleship course

4. *"It's Personal"* Daily Journal- A 90-day supply of our bestselling product will help you walk and talk with God

5. The *"It's Personal"* Journal CD- Explains how to use your journal to walk with God

6. The Ten Principles of Prosperity DVD- Over an hour of exciting teaching from Steve Curington on how to overcome addiction

order online ***www.reformu.com*** or call ***815-986-0460***

The Umbrella Fella
CE-123 $12.00

Within every believer's heart is a desire to be all that God would have us to be. But, how can we be what God wants us to be, when we cannot even do the things God wants us to do?! The Umbrella Fella will help us better understand our position in the kingdom of Heaven's chain of command. Once we understand our position, it will forever change our disposition. It all begins with a two letter preposition, the little word – IN.

order online **www.reformu.com** or call **815-986-0460**

Experience the Joy of Being -N-.

RU-N-TOUCH MINI-MAG

Subscribe to this powerful bi-monthly publication. It is filled with powerful articles on living a victorious Christian life, reaching the addicted, and developing God's power on your life. Don't go another day without this life-changing literature in your home or church. This is your direct link to the dynamic ministry of Reformers Unanimous International and its worldwide outreach!

❏ **$120 for Chapter Bundle** *(10 copies per issue)* ❏ **$ 20 One-Year Subscription**

❏ **$ 15 Subscription Renewal** *(One Year)*

order online *www.reformu.com* or call *815-986-0460*

RU is now 24/7
Check out Reformers Unanimous' online forum

Are you telling your Beginners' Class about the RU Forum? Have you told your leaders and students? If not, why? The forum is a place of healthy dialogue between students, leaders, and directors across America. Coupled with our internet savvy moderators, it is a safe place for the many people who look to this ministry for encouragement in their road to recovery. Do not assume that your voice is unnecessary. I would like more directors to post a fourth talk praise note of their Friday night class, and I would like to see more students signing on at least once a week to glorify God or to gain good insights from people in different stages of spiritual development. **–Bro. Curington**

• *Receive advice and ideas from students and directors around the world*
• *Read about encouraging testimonies of victory in the lives of other students*
• *Read postings from Steve Curington and Ben Burks*
• *Let others be encouraged by what God is doing in your RU*

Visit the forum today. *www.onlinebaptist.com/ru/*